WHERE RIVERS MEET

WHERE RIVERS MEET

BOB ARNOLD

MAD RIVER PRESS

Richmond, Massachusetts

ISBN 0-944156-04-5

First Edition

Library of Congress Cataloging in Publication Data is available.
LC Card number 89-13324

I am grateful to the following people and their presses where many of these poems first appeared in limited edition books: Charles and Pamela Plymell: Cherry Valley Editions: for *ROPE OF BELLS* (1974); Gary Lawless: Blackberry Press: *ALONG THE WAY* (1979); Michael Tarachow: Pentagram: *HABITAT* (1979), *THREAD* (1980), SELF-EMPLOYED (1983) and *GAZE* (1985); John Judson: Juniper Press: *BACK ROAD CALLER* (1985); Dennis Maloney: White Pine Press: *SKY* (1986); Barry Sternlieb: Mad River Press: *CACHE* (1987).

Magazines and anthologies: COUNTRY JOURNAL, EDGE (Japan), COYOTE'S JOURNAL, FALK (West Germany), FLUTE, HANDBOOK, HARPER'S, HEAVEN BONE, NEW LETTERS, ONE-HUNDRED POSTERS, PLOUGHSHARES, PORCH, SALT BLOCK, SALTED IN THE SHELL, SOLTIDE, SPOOR, and WHITE PINE JOURNAL.

FOR NERUDA, FOR CHILE, edited by Walter Lowenfels (Beacon Press).

AN EAR TO THE GROUND: An Anthology of Contemporary American Poetry edited by Marie Harris and Kathleen Aguero (The University of Georgia Press)

Cover graphic by Rita Corbin

Mad River Press
State Road
Richmond, Massachusetts 01254

for Susan & Carson

October : for Susan

It is a small bowl
You wash from
This early morning

Your hands just right
For its depth

Table of Contents

I *DAYS ALONE*

II *HABITAT*

III *WOODCUTTER*

IV *BACK ROAD CALLER*

WHERE RIVERS MEET

DAYS ALONE

I

TERRA

There is evidence of spring everywhere
A pair of geese, into a headwind / point north
The shed door shuts easier now
Rain water comes to the meadows
Planks are thrown down

PASSING

It is Spring
Already you relax in a cotton skirt
Passing through mountains is a strong feeling
Fields plowed, new wood split, a hawk floating
Puffs of softwood in the gray hills
A river runs with snow melting
A small bridge neatly built to get by
There is pleasure in such places
An old woman and her huge straw hat
Raking the far corner of a hayfield

FINDING OPEN WATER

There are these things
That make lovely creatures
More lovely—
A red-tailed hawk sweeps
From one moment of the hillside
To another
Rising mist will not lose him

3 deer wade into the shoulder of a field
They feel safe in the holler of rain

Then you, rolling up your pants
Before a bicycle ride
Your hair just touching the ground
I tell you I will do something with that
Your smile makes the beginning of all this

WALKING FROM TOWN BETWEEN MIDNIGHT AND 4 A.M.

I must have carried out
Every peeper in this valley

Home with me, 13 miles
Trees shiver in light rain

The moon following the
Fences following

A hillside of fog lies down
Generously in an apple orchard

Here is where a few sheep
Suddenly break into a run

A horse pounds the night
Meeting you at barbed wire

What is the sound between us
It is water that has brought me back

LAMP

After supper
No longer summer
A windy night ahead
We sit in the kitchen
One lamp
Read before the fire
Nothing else in our lives
Boots drying
Rain on the windows

HUMMINGBIRD

Rarely pausing
Though I have seen
It stop the flutter
Of its amazing
Wings and perch
Nearly invisible
On a wire against
The evening sky—
And be sighted—
And being very
Still, be thought
Of as not there

LOVE AND LANDSCAPE

Don't ask us how we crossed the saltwater marsh
Grasses were high and easy under foot
The last stream was spanned by a driftwood plank
Thrown carefully into the muck
I didn't sink and you didn't sink
And when we came to ocean
Skittering of sandpipers
You held your dress and walked into the spray
It must have been also the sudden daylight that I loved

LOSS

Put no trust in nothing, not even yourself
Yesterday was like summer, today snow blows
I've walked six miles with an axe and wedge
Actually make my living near a river running bright water
Home to a small hawk found mangled in the woodshed
Eyes opening, I load my rifle but won't use it
Instead talk with the closest thing to me right now
Heavy gloves moving back short feathers
The break in its neck, claws no use, eyes closing

VISITORS

The river for weeks is low
Visitors arrive
Call it a creek
We know better
Say nothing

Next month in a downpour
Bridges wash out
Trees go down
Days of mud
No one visits

WHAT I HEAR

This river water is
The warm breath of
Her whisper, what I hear—
The brown and white flurry
Of her thin clothing
The sweat of handwork
That musses the long
Blonde hair—dirt across
The forehead, may I wash
It off? thicken my hands
In that hair, kiss what I love
Away from our work and bathing
Part whisper and part water

ROPE OF BELLS

It is the
Rope of bells
You have put behind the door
That let me know
Whenever one of us goes
To the privy
The woodshed
The outdoors
Lovely

WINTER

Just before supper
I watched a storm draw in
Taking light
The trees toss
No matter
I have finished carrying
Elm from the edge of the woods
Bucked, split then stacked
I am done
Well used
Come snow

HOW WE BUILD

It is a day
Of sawing slab wood
Splitting
Then stacking
And be done

Tucking away insulation
Fixing windows
Sharpening every tool

The happy moment
Is there are still
Small grasshoppers
In the slip of meadow
That it is 28 degrees
At 7 this morning
And I wash your hair
In one bucket of
Strong spring water—
There is nothing like it

HABITAT

II

CHANGES

Under the waterfall
Leaves finally reach
Bottom and stay put,
Every known foliage
Puffed into a hive
May strike you dizzy
When the sun is on them
And water above flows
Clear, the shaken colors
Point into your eyes
First winter light

DOGS

With no more light
But for stars that have returned
After days unsettled, warm,
Now winter is here.
I walk out onto my small side porch
Just for its sake,
Short planks under me cracking cold,
To find the whole of a squirrel tail
Dark and smoke colored
Left there, somehow.

Better to leave it, and I did,
Soft without touching—
Closed the door
The fire down
Animals that kill, peacefully asleep.

MUCH OF MY OWN LIFE

It is a sad thing, but true,
Out of 6 ducks, one female,
The smallest of males
Will be singled out and
Pecked upon until weakness.
It may take us months to
Notice this, thinking it
More playing—
And when it is almost too late
We will gather straw with an empty
Melon box and close to the fire
It will nest, try to live.
Somehow the large dog and stray cat
Meet the arrangements—
And day after day this bird
Will turn in its tumbled setting,
Feathers green, blue and gray
Watch me for hours, I swear.

BOBOLINK

He watches my entry
Down the tilt of pasture
Clumps of mud sinking rubber boots,
Chain saw load and fuel jugs,
Holds an eye on me
In his one position.
When I set to work he sets to work,
Drops off the long spring of telephone wire.
Through the day picks at brush piles, goes
Back onto the wire, withstands the heat, watches.
It is only when the saw is shut down I hear what
He says, the scale of whistles both sharp
And gentle to the ear, no one pitch alike, perhaps
The voice of many birds together, in this one who
Peers down as I leave and now starts to sing.

TURNING THE PAGE

Dear Stephen Carlson, I'm writing you
Because you aren't here anymore, but
In the 119th Annual Town Report for this
Year I'm reminded of your name and
What it is all about. You demolished
In your VW traveling home from work
One night from out here where the hills
Roll. My neighbor tells me you were
Building yourself up quite a herd of cows
And were the honest type and hard working,
Night after night milking in the long barn
Lights up off Weatherhead Hollow Road.
22 years old and they killed you, doesn't
Make much sense. Four headlights drag
Racing right at you and the scream that
Came from your voice is something you
Never knew you had—and now your wife
Of 4-months owns it and all dreams are
Nightmares—and I'm trying to do my best
For you, as only one maybe can, as I turn
The booklet tonight from page 51, which has
Printed your death, to page 52, which makes
Note to your marriage.

TREEPLANTER

Never see how—
But see how—
The pine tree
Has grown a foot
Since a year ago

SKY

Hiking down from a hillside
Snow packed, saw on the shoulder
There is no doubt now
Of rain in the air
I stop at a sound
Far / nearing / wait
Two crows flying
Calling, wide apart
One straight south
The other—eastward
Belly on the tree line
I've lost sight of one
For keeping with the other

ON BUILDING A STONEWALK IN NOVEMBER

This river drifts the land,
In the long air of pines
I smell spring.
Down here, don't wear gloves,
Don't wear boots with leaks,
Stay working, and of course
Use the flat stones—
All the things
One learns
In a first year—
The boots take awhile, I know.
But come to your water gentle,
Very clear
Draw strong
Carry the river home to bathe.
It is November / wide open / colding
There is ice you shouldn't trust.

DOG MEAT

Up on the hill where the sun warms
Under thick maples he used to
Pull a sled of sap buckets past,
I'd see him right there as I walked the road
Pastured in a circle of stamped snow,
Content with hay and pail of oats—
Soft brown except where the hooves
Bushed long white hairs.
Never seemed to move from that place
Though his eyes would see me from a distance,
Wait and turn his head as I went by—
We would look at one another, and I
Remember it very clear today as I pass
And he's nowhere around—
Sold for $350 I found out later.
The first time in seven years
I haven't nodded to him my hello,
And this walk isn't the same.

SELF-EMPLOYED

Take two squared stones and
Drop them almost side by side
Lift the thinner slab of rock and
Bust your guts setting it on top
Now you got reason to sit down

SUGARHOUSE GONE

You'd think it would have
Lasted forever like some
Of them around here do—
This one halfway nested
Beneath the ground, piled
On stone. Downstairs, then
Empty of buckets, if you looked
Above between wide floor boards
You would see where tubs
Of sap are brought to boil
And a few souls go at it day and night
In this tiny place with windows lit,
And open shutters of the cupola
Dieseling clouds of sweet steam
Had you at some point in the day
Lean for a cooling moment out the
Sugarhouse door—feeling a realness
In yourself, the redwing's flight over
Steep pasture, dry mud on high boots—
All of this for warm days and cold nights.
While the fire that bubbled your syrup
Was somehow the same fire
That burned you down.

REAL LIFE

It was a hot day thrown suddenly cool
By that hard rain, poured off the slate roof barn
When the boy was hit by lightning.
Standing safe, he thought, in the large doorway,
Eaves above him tapping,
Farm trucks shining up.
Big for his age, father's overalls, watching things,
Whole complexion tan like pure maple syrup
The stuff he gathered with his grandfather and horses.
His old man and older brothers stoke and boil the woodfire,
Spend those long nights in the sugarhouse.
The way light spills out of the small steamy windows
All over snow, dreamy in the valley.

Well a mean bolt came down from the sky to end that,
A splitting axe flying.
Water dripping smooth from the roof edge
Splashes onto his boots and cuffs,
Hayseed still itching his back,
Cows poking behind him in their stalls.
Need a light already it's getting so dark, he thought—
Struck him from the forehead straight down
Cracked him open like nothing should be.
The family dog lay nearby on a broken bale
Like he has for 15 Julys,
Large head on his paws tilted and watching
Rain burning the ground.

IT'S SO

After love, you lift your dress
Wash in cold running water.
I've to work in the morning,
Drive through the field, frighten
A flicker from wet grass
To the stone wall, birch, white oak.
It all started with you hugging my neck
Pulling back and laughing.
We'd open a large window upstairs
Lie down in the river sound.

The mason's young helper unloads stone
Then breaks for a cigarette,
All day guns cement mixer blades.
Long handle shovel stuck in sand
Lime dust blowing
Whitewash peeling from ripped out
Barn ceiling boards.
Two weeks ago this was a new job—
Rotten sills weren't jacked
Bolts cut—
A buzzard flew up from the valley
Cockeyed in stiff wind
Beating rough edged wings,
Very black on melting snow.

Now 4-wheel drives burn tread
On the hillside, tool boxes slam
Workers pitch vision to the ground,
Black flies sting our skin.

By the end of day a red fox
Hops out of that sunny part of the field.
I hear a schoolbus downshift miles away.
Two guys clean out a wheelbarrow
Drink from the hose
Talk of bear hunting.

FARAWAY, LIKE THE DEER'S EYES

for Victor Jara, Chilean folksinger

Ah yes, now I believe I know—
A cool breeze and very early morning
A wood thrush breaks from the pasture,
Fences have all been mended,
Here and there animal hair.

I think of Jara; Victor,
By jesus as they busted your fingers
And you kept to the last moment
Something loving, say your sister, far in your belly.
Then they beat you like the backside of a horse
And it all fell—my chore bucket spilled
Suddenly in Vermont.

I may still have the gathering of birds,
The pull of this long river
Where I wade to my waist, undo my hair and wash slowly
Strong sweat and black flies,
A quiet day with the saw
Now near its end.

But Chile stays—forever.
How in the hell can you ask me to forget
A father dragged down from an attic
And pumped into a scream
In front of his huddled family?
The blood goes everywhere
And they live with it
And the killers—shit,
Something the raccoon wouldn't even wash.

Daylight goes.
Evening is soon.
My friends, we are to become
The last light in the pond.

WOODCUTTER

III

NIGHT TABLE

Here is part of you
While you sleep—

The small shine
Of silver earrings

DOGS IN SNOW

I bring them out water
They drink around the ice
Chains rap on the bucket

Shivering I wait
Looking up into the stars
What I see in their eyes

Plowing back to the house
After shaking their coats goodnight
Strength in my hands

THE PLEASURES OF LOVE

The last of my noon hour
Black tin lunch pail
Sitting on a sap soaked maple stump
Woodchips nettled on my woolen socks
Finding a fruit cup she made for me
Clear cold glass in my oiled hand
Neat slices of strawberry and pear

DECEMBER

She's supposed to be land clearing
Heaping brush to burn in first snow
But the pale yellow ghost of tall
Summer grasses she sweeps down
Is instead caught in her hand
And placed that way in a kitchen vase
Showing a warmth to last us through winter

WORK GLOVES

On the garden gate
Left here with me—
Shape of her hands

I HAVE BEEN TOLD

Down on the river
There is a small place
Where there is no sound
Nothing, and I know it well
And I have been told
And since found
That when climbing back
Loaded with water
At the top of the rise
If you half turn your head
The river will tilt into your ear

HORSE & FARMHAND

Here is the slowness
Of afternoon and sun
A farmhand bending to lift
A sleeve of ice
From a trough
In the pasture
The horse that stands still
The snow we've been waiting for

WINTER DAY

I swore if you laid
Your cheek, wind
Blown red as any
Soft maple leaf
Onto the pond,
And looked down through
The half-foot of
Ice, the rest was
Water flowing clear
Way back up to you—
The scales of depth
Catching your breath

MANY TIMES

There is the absolute way
Of doing it, and we have done it
Many times and again—
How I will come to you
How you will meet me
The early morning sun
Perfect on the bed, and
Stripes in the Mexican blanket
Like blood, the sea, yellow iris petals—
And it is a silly lovers ritual of ours,
I hug you and you hug me and step onto
My boots, and I walk you and me around the
Sunlit room, the sway of patchouli in your hair,
And your face smooth against my lips
Like the inside of your hands

THE SKIN OF HER NECK

Tonight, because her hand
Is in pain, the small finger
Swollen, yes, I'll stir the
Batter, although she is better
And first taught me how
Something is done right.
And I came from behind
And smelled the skin of
Her neck, the long blonde
Hairs alive and the blouse
White and rough, tucked into
A thin summer skirt.
Winter, near Christmas,
3 feet of snow and her
Body moves across the
Cabin room with summer,
A clay bowl with
Colored stripes in her
Arms, the fresh heat
Of the flat iron stove.

REDTAIL

By the river I found her—
Long and short feathers matted by weeks of rain,
A soft spotted down on her chest,
The whole body twisted in the crotch of an ironwood
This hawk hung and not a right way to die.
Nudged out with my axe handle it fell with no life,
Eyes gone and the rotting smell of blood and grease.
I cut the claws for the first time, other's I've left—
One talon broken off and the muscular flex of skin
No different than a man's, except for the ruggedness,
The pale yellow of it, but a companion to my own.
And the tail feathers—still a beautiful tan—pinned
Open for flight on rough pine boards inside our cabin,
I only buried some of her.

THE WOODCUTTER TALKS

I've got to go pretty soon
So I'll take my boots off
And shake out the snow,
Sit close to the fire you
Have built, then left for me.
I'm in no hurry until the sun comes up.
My snowshoes need new leather straps
But for now they'll have to do,
Carry me to the woods where I work
Thinning out the half bowl of a hillside—
That's what it looks like—and sometimes
I rest and watch it for what it is, with my
Wet gloves off, the clearness above me.

BACK ROAD CALLER

IV

FARMER'S WIFE

Four dozen eggs under her arm,
That's how she greeted us.
We weren't coming for eggs
But for a currant bush
Waiting in the dooryard
Wrapped tight in burlap.
I lifted it into the back
Of the truck since that's
What I was hired to do,
Waited in the early sun
Leaning against the tailgate
While the two old ladies talked.
And with the eggs still under
Her arm she also turned to speak
With me, eyes dazzled like light
In water, checkered blue flannel
Shirt, out-worn by all of her
Sons and now on her back; torn
At the elbows, but warm.
Everything is just right
On this hill farm and I've only
Been here 5 minutes. Crows flap
West to east from the wood's edge
Long over the flat face of pasture.
A manure spreader is backed up
To the kitchen door stacked neat
With stovewood, the lawn is mowed,
And we've caught this farmer's wife

In between the chicken coop and
The house; white hair combed back
With ruddy hands that pick eggs
Each morning, and when she talks
She mentions all of her family.

CLAYTON

Clayton always had a pricky word
To say about the hippies.
They lived in a commune
Over the hill from his farm.
He ran into them at three places
At any one time during the year—
Either when he was hunting the hill
As he did every year for 40 years,
Or when he was running his snow-machine
On the back roads.
Finally he would see them in town
Every other Friday, when he was
Cashing his check from the state park.
And they was always cashing
Some other kind of check,
Smiling at him.

Of course I was a hippie to Clayton too
Because I had the long beard,
But we worked together when he came home
To his farm on the river.
Helped him screed the foundation floor
Under his house and lay down the roof, too—
Fix fence, cut the firewood and solder sap pails.
But one day I'll never forget
Was when we were haying the lower mowings in August—
His wife had moved out long ago
And he was living with his son
And the big TV antenna.
But these summer days were spent
A long time haying,

Waiting on the weather
And broken down farm machines.

We had just finished up work,
Had the trailer swayed down loaded
With 200 bales and were coming around
The bend near the second swimming hole
When Clayton caught sight of something
Standing fresh out open
In the shallow part of the river—
A young woman soaping herself
And blonde naked as pine lumber,
Sunlight enshrined in the water
Around her knees.
We both stared like idiots
Until we got broadside with her,
Then we looked straight ahead
Business as usual
But I know she didn't move.

Further up the road
Clayton twisted his sunburned neck
And skinny white t-shirt
Around in the tractor seat,
Looked back where I was
Holding onto the trailer stakes
And hollered: "I never did mind the hippie women!"

FARLOW

Just imagine Farlow
On Washington's Birthday
When he came out the back door
Into his woodshed and caught
Clayton's small hunting-pup
Digging through his trash.
According to the story
He told the game warden
Was that the pup attacked him,
So he had to shoot it.

Clayton never bought that story.
He knew from past experience
Of his own that Farlow's wife
Had left him six months
After they moved here from Connecticut.
He was spending weekend nights
And now weekdays
In bars in town after work,
Might have even brought home a lady,
But most probably not.

Clayton could read Farlow's house lights
A quarter-mile away from where
He sat nights in his kitchen—
No houses in-between.
If he used the scope of his rifle
He could even see more.
As winter sunk in
Farlow was keeping odd-hours—

Arriving home late,
Wandering around the house weekends,
And shooting his rifle off for hours
In his field on Sunday afternoons.
The house was said to have an arsenal—
Maybe 30 rifles and pistols for one man—
And it only took one to shoot the dog.

After that, Clayton didn't deal with him,
Didn't pay attention to his house lights,
And in turn Farlow leased out his hayfield
To someone else, instead of Clayton—
First time in years.

Since then both men have remarried,
Moved away, and the house of Farlow's
Was bought by a millionaire gentleman farmer.
I still hear Farlow target practicing
In his field on a Sunday afternoon,
Even though he is long gone.
Clayton's son says they have so many puppies
Around at his father's old place
That they'll probably have to drown a few of them
In the river this spring.

WARM

Apple, poplar, ash,
Cherry, red maple,
Pine, basswood, oak,
These are the woods
That we sawed today.
In two hours of thinning,
Selecting, we made a cord—
Trampled branches on snow
Worked without words.
Simple thoughts, like picking
Up these sticks—back and
Forth in the mind—until we
Stop to rest together against
The pile, brushing off woodchips,
Shedding hats and gloves,
And because we kiss, I warm
My hands beneath your blouse.

FIRST SNOW AS I SPLIT WOOD

Thin snow falling into
Valley fog, quiets everything,
No bird call, nothing flying.
The splitting wedge and hammer
Echo over the pasture
While the flakes open bigger
For no reason other than snow.
And I straighten my sweaty back
To watch this world, lend a tongue
And taste it melt.

SCOUT

Here you are again
Late at night
Snow falling in the valley
Life on snowshoes

Hardly faraway from home
In fact, isn't that the glow
Of the kitchen lamp
Lighting through the trees

I've spent the better part
Of darkness stamping in
A mile wide circle enjoying
The measure of going nowhere

Stand with me
Waste some time
Everything you've always wanted
Is all around you.

NOW

Without any warning,
No wind or dampness,
Just as I was about to
Step out from under
The empty barn stall,
Shake woodchips
After chain saw work
From my rubber boots
Then split the wood—
Sleet rained down all at once
As if someone whispered *now*
Caught even the chickadees
Feeding in the overgrown
Raspberry canes, but I
Watched as they regained
Themselves over the
Pasture, flying away.

THE LONG WAY HOME

January and no thaw
Freezing days and nights
Far back in the woods
I stamped caked ice
Off my snowshoes after
Breaking into the open
Onto an old logging road

Returning down into the valley
Sunlight rinsing the hills
Passing my neighbor's pasture
I feel staring between the trees
Huddled in deep snow
The whole world stop
As horses watch

ONE SHOT

for Russell Denison

The one shot
I don't think
He wanted to shoot
Put this deer down,
Found on the river ice
After the dogs
Had been chased off.

He left the body alive
Longer than I would
For someone to call
The game warden, or
Hoping 3 or 4 in the pack
Would circle back,
Put a slug in each one's head.

But nothing returned—
This deer waits
Head flat
Muscles clawed from her legs,
She won't ever rise again.
Bloody dog tracks
Pinwheeled from the body.

It is late winter
An open sunny day for a change,
The air is starting to melt
With new bird songs—
Her eyes are wide
She can't move
Watches us as we move.

SUGARING TIME

All at once
Off in the distance
Where an old hut
Sinks into the ground
Two small windows lit
And steam bellows
Up into the farmland sky—
You thought it was a fire
Until you tasted the air

JACK BELDEN

Uncle Jack is what the young kids
Around here call him, even though he
Isn't really their uncle but rather
Their own parents' uncle and usually
They just call him Jack. His name
Doesn't come up too much when I'm
Working with my neighbors.
There are three houses of the same family
Up the dirt road running alongside
French Brook. The brook eventually
Climbs higher into the next town of
Cheshire and Jack drinks from this brook.
The dirt road winds around Church Mountain
And swings back into the village
Passing through the covered bridge
And over the waterfall,
Forking then into two roads like a wishbone
That provides travel for a dozen families.
They hardly ever come down our road
Which follows the river, and I don't
Think anyone knows Jack Belden up there.

The three houses on Jack's back road
Are the homes for two of his nephews
And his sister; Jack's small trailer
Is hidden in a hollow from them all.
He never married, doesn't own a car,
Hikes to Brattleboro 12 miles away or
Picks up a ride with the rural mailtruck.

One day walking home from work
I was 500 feet behind Jack who had just
Left the mailtruck in the covered bridge
And was stalking down the muddy river road.
Middle of the season. A warm day.
The buckets on the roadside maples
Brimming with sap.
A mile down the road
And still a distance between us
I watched him abruptly stop,
Look both ways (but not behind him),
Let down his burlap sack of groceries
From his shoulder, then walk to
One of the trees and remove a bucket,
Drink for a good half-minute
Wipe his mouth with his sleeve
Hang the bucket back
Then continue the remaining mile to home.
I thought all about that yesterday—
It was eight years ago. He was 75 years old.

Today I'm tapping the same trees
On the farmer's land Jack drank from.
The mud is deep and the day is warm,
Not much has changed.
But I heard and couldn't believe
That Jack has been in the hospital
Since January, the month we broke
All records for freezing temperatures.
I recall one night sitting with neighbors
Already reminiscing about
The headaches of busted water pipes
Depleting cordwood and icy roads,
But no talk about Jack—
The whiskered old man who walks.

Everett, his nephew, told me
As we filled our aprons with tap spouts
That Jack's gas ran out in the trailer
During one of those real cold nights.
30 below. His feet froze.
They amputated the gangrene from all his toes.
Shut out all the lights to any more walking.

I wonder what this all means—
We worry about water pipes bursting,
But a quarter-mile away
Jack loses his toes.
It wasn't brought up at town meeting this year.
Jack's photograph doesn't grace
The inside town report bulletin
As one of the patriarchs of Guilford.
Yet, he knows his territory—
Takes a leak outside his trailer door
Like any liberated yankee.
Quietly living so that you
Don't know that he lives.
Showed me once how to
Crush an early shad bud
Between my fingers
For the first scent of spring.

QUILLS

He didn't move—
With pliers I
Pulled 16 of them
From mouth, lips,
Nose and head—
Like last year
It is early spring

HEMLOCK

When the big hemlock
Washed down river
During one of the early
Spring runoffs, I went
Down with bowsaw and
Sawed off one large
Limb for the cabin
Steps handrail, and then
Went back and brought
Home a dozen smaller branches
Thinking they could be
Used for something—
Although they have only
Stood up behind the woodshed,
Bleaching in the sun,
Warping away from
Straighter timber
They once knew.

FRIEND

This sparrow must
Love the sun—
All day it has perched
On the stone well
Beside the empty
Trough of seed

All day its feathers
Lifted in the breeze

Its head turning
The oddest angles

If I could have him
He would fit in
The palm of my hand

BLOSSOMS

Beneath rain clouds
She wheelbarrows
Loose black soil
Of daylilies
From the brook
To plant around
A ledge of stone
And in a month
She will smell like
The yellow blossoms

PRIZE

Away from the road,
Off into the high edge
Of a field, unless I
Looked carefully you
Would never have been seen
Picking wildflowers
Growing in folds of sunlight
Among the tall grass.

Each snipped by hand
At the same height, then
Gathered inside a pail
Of shallow water.

The world seems weightless
Watching you work,
If this is work—
You call it a prize
Saved for the last
Hour of the afternoon,
Taking away what this
Plot of land has to give—
Flowers for the kitchen table,
Brightened windowsills.

DAY AND NIGHT

How often have we
Stepped together into water—
You left your clothes on the rocks
And shivered your way to me,
Said it was freezing as I thought
Of the mountain stream filling this
Clear basin of evening light, and how
Swallows showed us the angles of the sky
Far above barbed wire and pasture heat
Which we came down from after work
Smelling lilac in the breeze—
And it was the long blonde hair you shook
Out of a blue bandana and later braided
That had me remember the day and night.

HANDS

He was the first
One ever to show
Me anything, and
Make sense, about
A garden. When he
Called me down into
The fenced half-acre
I walked through the
Wire gate and found
Him shoulder high
In the early morning
Blossom of peas.
And snapping a pod
Open, with the same
Hands that cut timber,
Mended fence and
Milked cows—who
Came in here every
Morning before he
Went off to chores —
He put everything
Into my hands
When he said,
Now taste this.

HEREABOUTS

for Jim Koller

The town is acting proud,
Even a photograph in the newspaper,
Everyone I talk to hereabouts
Has something to say about
The bear that was shot nearby.

I haven't really pinned down
Where it was killed, but one
Mile between us and the radius
Of the valley seems a fair account.
That would include across the river,
Up the incline of timber to
Owl's Head Range, where three winters
In a row we would hear probably
The same bear rumbling around
In this box of territory left to roam.

Funny noises he makes, hoots
And barks, moans with long silence.
We listened. No better than
The next guy, just listened
To a sound you don't hear
Too much of any longer hereabouts.
Like the golden eagle over
West River last spring, ice going out
I stood there where I was working,
Chain saw shut down quiet,
Watching the bird float above the day—
You miss it when it's gone.

WALK TO THE BARN

All of life, even the mountains
Around him are changing.

Yet he walks twice each day
To the barn up the wide gravel drive,

No more cattle inside.
His slow and steady pace

Pays respect to the surrounding pasture,
The ring of woodland and evening birds.

What once made him prosperous
Is now gone, except for what he loves—
His wife, old dog, farm buildings and land.
He leans open the heavy sliding barn door,

Steps out of view.

AT THE COUNTRY WEDDING

They don't tinkle
Champagne glasses
With their spoons here
And only the old folks
Are sitting down.
A country western group
Has lugged its equipment upstairs,
And later today and into the evening
This young married couple
Will learn the sweet
And rotten joys
From the masters of it—
Dancing fathers and mothers,
Lonesome aunts and yodeling uncles.
But for the moment
Paper plates are heaped with
Homemade ham, biscuits and beans
And all a few people want
Is a kiss,
So tapping on the side
Of a beer bottle with a knife
Quiets the whole grange hall down
Into love.

HUNTER

Late in the afternoon
This farmer drove his tractor
Across the river, broke open the thin ice,
Put out salt in the bare ground mowing
And if you looked, you could find his
Red jacket working behind the trees.

That night edges of the river froze again.
Big bright stars burned cold over the hills.
I was carrying in cookstove wood
For the next morning
When the gunshot shook down valley,
Then back up.

Two days later a farm dog
Held the deer's head
Where he lay down
Chained to the barn.

SENIOR CITIZEN

Probably 1,000 carpenters
Live in the southern part
Of this state, a lot of them
Hip and young with a brand new
Leather apron, heavy duty
Trucks, wives or companions
That are weavers or potters
Or dancers, and of course they
All have a story to tell.
Though yesterday I was in
An old woman's house high off
From the back road, and she
Lived alone and missed all
Her grandchildren and braided
Rugs in the back of the house
With a hand needle and years
And years of wool, and the
Story she had to tell was
Already written in her choice
Of words, the rope of her hands,
And the scar above her left eye
Made thirty-five years ago
By the shuttle of a textile loom.

BACK ROAD CALLER

I came to have my chain saw fixed
And he did that, but
A half hour job
Stretched to three hours
Because he had to show me
All his new tools,
Plus his 75lb. bow
And the antlers from the buck
He shot last fall—
"Arrow went clean through"
Never mind the drawer
Of chewing tobacco
He offered me, and then
To his father, and we both
Politely declined a dip,
And as if that wasn't enough—
He pulled out the flat
Enveloped reeds he used
For turkey hunting—
Tucked one up on the roof
Of his mouth and cupping
His hands chucked out a
Perfect few syllables
Which would have turned any
Bird's head, and depending
On how he rolled his body
With a call he could make
It sound horny, but he
Only saved that one for
The summertime, when the
Weekend neighbor's daughter
Came to visit all alone.

APPROACH

I've only been away one day
But already between the width
Of the stone wall gate
Spans the thinnest first strand of
A spider's web, floating there
As the river fog this morning
In the valley—well enough to
Stoop beneath it,
Cause no harm.

ABOVE THE VALLEY

for Scott Tindall

Over 3,000 feet
Above the valley
Our eyes looking
Southward with an
Old man we came
Upon resting on a
Stump. We exchanged
Greetings in the warm
Light he enjoyed,
The leaves falling,
And asked where
He had hiked from.
And he stood up and
Pointed to a lake I knew
Far off in the lower hills
Catching the sun, saying
"The other lake after that"—
One I never knew of.
Then later in the day
Higher up from the old man,
Air sharp with balsam,
We looked back and saw how
His lake had lit up too.

MARSH HAWK

Only 10 yards
Away, and I
Didn't see her

Fly there, and
I won't see
Her fly off—

Feathers matching
Down into the
Gray rain
Cedar post

Eyes looking
Straight ahead
Staring me down

SHIRT IN THE WOODS

It was a shirt in the woods,
He's worn it all week
Pulled out cordwood with me—
Broke his truck down twice,
Climbed under and fixed it—
Drove the family to town
For supper at the Burger King
And wore the same shirt.
Said maybe his father had left it
On a tree the week before while
Cutting logs, or a hunter had walked
Through and forgot about it.
That's his logic, makes sense.
Found over a low beech branch—
Tufted flannel, doggy, typical—
The same color these hills are
After the beautiful leaves have dropped.

NO TOOL OR ROPE OR PAIL

It hardly mattered what time of year
We passed by their farmhouse,
They never waved,
This old farm couple
Usually bent over in the vegetable garden
Or walking the muddy dooryard
Between house and red-weathered barn.
They would look up, see who was passing,
Then look back down, ignorant to the event.
We would always wave nonetheless,
Before you dropped me off at work
Further up on the hill,
Toolbox rattling in the backseat,
And then again on the way home
Later in the day, the pale sunlight
High up in their pasture,
Our arms out the window
Cooling ourselves.
And it was that one midsummer evening
We drove past and caught them sitting
Together on the front porch
At ease, chores done,
The tangle of cats and kittens
Cleaning themselves of fresh spilled milk
On the barn door ramp;
We drove by and they looked up—
The first time I've ever seen their
Hands free of any work,
No tool or rope or pail—
And they waved.

SEASONS

V

DRUM

Early morning climb to the roof
Cold dew on pebbled tar, taste of
Galvanized nails in your mouth
Work—nail shingle to shingle tight—
Each hammer pound echoes another
Pound in the hills, enough to wonder
Where it ends and who hears it then

CHARLOTTE

Scrag is what they call her.
A woman who has been on the river
Longer than anyone of us—
Long white hair braided and pinned up,
Yellow slicker, old pants and a squint.
Once a week she rides down the road
Real slow to the Massachusetts border,
Looks in on everyone's place,
Then turns around and coming back
Does the same.
Her son doesn't live out here anymore—
When Clayton did, he lost his wife for it.
Lived with his son and the small farm
For as many years as it takes to get
Sick of it, then moved closer to town
And worked for the state park.
Now his own son is doing the same—
With a wife and a baby and the job
In a wood factory, near Vernon,
Where the power plant burns into the sky.

That leaves Scrag.
I heard that name first from a young hunter
Who would never hunt, half what she has,
And he knows it.
She's tiny, body gripped like hickory,
She'll tend the farm all men have left—
Mend fence and draw water and shovel shit,
Make sure the pigs don't get loose.

When Clayton comes to sugar at mud-time
She hangs the buckets with him,
Pulls a tractor along the side of the road.
Her hair's long and white and probably beautiful.
In this raw wind it blows apart like late summer
Milkweed.

TREEING THE RACCOON

I'm running and dodging mud holes
And ice, a human wind slamming out of
The woodshed and into moonlight,
Where we have lain and waited the
Return of the raccoon. I was thinking
Of grabbing a coal shovel, the axe,
Even a stick on my way out the door,
But my voice seemed to do the trick—
Frightening him off tin sheets of
The duck pen and into the darkness of
His mask. I'm crushing through soft snow
And somewhere ahead he's scurrying it
Seems in a half-circle, until my war cry
Has gripped him claws and bark up a
Tall ash tree between the house and pond—
Maybe 20 feet—until he has regained
Himself in the crotch; where under the
Wizard cap of stars I poke a flashlight
Into the first night of spring, and with
A disgusted look in the eye, he turns his
Ears back and waits a bullet I can't hear.

THIS PLACE IN EVERY LIFE

for John Levy

A span of 20 feet—
Someone, but no
One's around, once
Laid down these log
Poles and nailed the
Planks for what I balance
On and cross, and then
Turn and once again
Walk over, because I
Like the feeling, a
Mountain creek beneath
And leaves floating,
The range of light—
Now back across slowly
The last time
Finally into my direction

BEEN GONNA

To Everett everything
He had meant to do was
Termed "been gonna"—
So when you view his
Unfinished farm built on top
Of old farms of the
Past, including the burned
Down house his was above,
And the barn once torched,
Never mind the wrecked cars
Over the river bank and
Sculptures of rusted farm
Machinery pulled into one
Corner of the pasture, and
The sugarhouse built on a
Slipping log sill, and the
Barbed wire fence line
Fallen in the brook, you're
Looking at a lot of been gonna.

PURPLE JAPANESE IRIS

Where you stand
They just about
Touch your lips

DOE

Standing midriver
Sunlight already
In the waves, long
Before any sound or
Movement beyond her
Own or my own—
Out of my clothes into
The water, looking up
I see her then, eyes
Meeting in the current
No sound I say, even as
She lifts her muzzle and
Rears her spotted hide
The stare lasts for years

SAND DOLLAR

We've waited all year
And traveled all morning
Just to arrive like this—
In the very same place
We were a year ago today.
And you are just as beautiful,
Your long skirt blowing in sand,
And we walk for miles along
The edge of the leaving tide
Picking up seashells and stone
That we'll select more carefully
The longer we are here—
Which is no place with a name,
Except someplace in our heart.
Where that day, unlike any other,
You found excitedly a sand dollar
Washed in during the night,
Left in a tidal pool, and
Kneeling while taking it up,
Placed it home in my hand.

PACIFIC

Lovelier—
When the
Bandana from
My pocket is
Worn around
Her neck

GHOSTS

March comes and water moves,
The river, ponds, brooks open.
On snowshoes this is the last week
You'll hike down these banks of
Rotten snow, the last week bridges
Of ice will be there to criss-cross
Down stream, the last week a
Deer carcass will be pinned between
Rocks and white water spray through
The white of her skull—the runoff
Will let her go, or break her to pieces—
You're aware of this where you step.
Pools of water swirl 5 feet deep,
Maybe her bones will lay down in the
Sand and white pebbles here, it is
The last week to think of any of this.
Beneath your feet of oblong ashwood
And softened leather you sense the newness
Of life—hide has slipped all winter off
The body, it is time to go places.

BARRED OWL

for Janine Pommy Vega

Without a sound
I made myself walk
A day in the sun
The thin pale grass breeze
An axe along to trim dead limbs

Moving beneath pines
I stopped when I saw its wings
Spread straight for me and
Grip itself 10 yards away
With no idea we were face to face

Black water of the eyes opening and seeing
Spotting easily what wasn't right

In a skiff of wind
She dropped and floated
Low to the ground
Lost my eye in blending flight
With feathers like the woodland

RISING

Some sound outside has raised our heads
Made us look into the eyes of one another.
You by the kerosene lamp glowing into your
Face and hair, knitting needles down in your lap.
I pull on high boots and wool shirt
Walk out to the dogs on their chains
Muzzles sniffing to the hillside.
We wait, beneath a clear wash of moonlight,
For sure we've heard something and we'll freeze
To hear it again—there, low bark, speaking from
A darkness left in the woods, excites the malamute
To circle his hut, piss on the pine he's tied under.
No stir or movement up there, though these barks are
Moving across the face of the night, striking out
From some loss or pain, wearing down a trail.

I leave the dogs whining to go to the river
Rushing deep and flashing white light of the sky.
This is the clearest night yet for October
Frost webs open ground
Deer everywhere must be fattening on mushed apples.
A howl, now straight across from me—
I can't see the bear but know it's a bear,
The call it makes fills that body.
In a moment it will be farther away
Gone back into the hairs of darkness.
I hear nothing more, as if I've heard enough—
Now the middle of the night.
Soon that white light will rise out of the river.

SEASONS

All my life
Lived under the stars,
Walked with them night after
Night, and I'm still
Learning how they move
Through the seasons.
And you help—point your
Gloved hand this winter
Evening almost over our heads
To Cassiopeia and then arc
To the North Star in the
Little of the dippers. It's
Easy once you know, once you
Are shown, once you have
Someone to see with.

© Jeff Kruh

While self-employed as a stonemason and builder, Bob Arnold's books of poetry have appeared regularly since 1974. In addition, he edits and publishes *Longhouse* books and journal. Born and raised in the Berkshire Hills of Massachusetts, Bob has made a home for many years in Vermont with his wife Susan and their son Carson.